MW01534120

HYDROPONICS

By Jim Gears

Copyright © 2017 by Jim Gears

All Rights Reserved. This document is geared towards providing exact and reliable information in regards to the topic and issue covered. The publication is sold with the idea that the publisher is not required to render accounting, officially permitted, or otherwise, qualified services. If advice is necessary, legal or professional, a practiced individual in the profession should be ordered.

- From a Declaration of Principles which was accepted and approved equally by a Committee of the American Bar Association and a Committee of Publishers and Associations.

In no way is it legal to reproduce, duplicate, or transmit any part of this document in either electronic means or in printed format. Recording of this publication is strictly prohibited and any storage of this document is not allowed unless with written permission from the publisher. All rights reserved.

The information provided herein is stated to be truthful and consistent, in that any liability, in terms of inattention or otherwise, by any usage or abuse of any policies, processes, or directions contained within is the solitary and utter responsibility of the recipient reader. Under no circumstances will any legal responsibility or blame be held against the publisher for any reparation, damages, or monetary loss due to the information herein, either directly or indirectly.

Respective authors own all copyrights not held by the publisher.

The information herein is offered for informational purposes solely, and is universal as so. The presentation of the information is without contract or any type of guarantee assurance.

The trademarks that are used are without any consent, and the publication of the trademark is without permission or backing by the trademark owner. All trademarks and brands within this book are for clarifying purposes only and are the owned by the owners themselves, not affiliated with this document.

Disclaimer and Terms of Use: The Author and Publisher has strived to be as accurate and complete as possible in the creation of this book, notwithstanding the fact that he does not warrant or represent at any time that the contents within are accurate due to the rapidly changing nature of the Internet. While all attempts have been made to verify information provided in this publication, the Author and Publisher assumes no responsibility for errors, omissions, or contrary interpretation of the subject matter herein.

Any perceived slights of specific persons, peoples, or organizations are unintentional. In practical advice books, like anything else in life, there are no guarantees of results. Readers are cautioned to rely on their own judgment about their individual circumstances and act accordingly.

This book is not intended for use as a source of legal, medical, business, accounting or financial advice. All readers are advised to seek services of competent professionals in the legal, medical, business, accounting, and finance fields.

TABLE OF CONTENTS

Chapter 1
What Is Hydroponics 5

Chapter 2
Choosing Hydroponics Medium 9

Chapter 3
Types Of Hydroponic System 32

Chapter 4
Plant Nutrition 36

Chapter 5
Lighting Solution 40

Chapter 6
Conclusion 43

CHAPTER I
WHAT IS HYDROPONICS

One of the branches of agriculture that has piqued the interest of gardening enthusiasts and hobbyist is known as Hydrophonics. To simplify it is the practice of growing various species of plants without using soil. In the absence of a dirt medium, a water solution that contains the nutrients plants need is put in place. Since plants require nutrients to grow, all the essentials are dissolved in water so that the roots can absorb what they need. Such systems are ideal in settings wherein there is limited space for the typical set up of growing plants on pots filled with nutrient-rich soil.

The origin of the term "hydrophonics" can be traced back to the Greek word for "water" (hydros) and "work" (ponos). The practice is becoming popular because of the decline in the availability of land for food production. Hydro systems are relevant today because the population growth rate continues to increase and the available land for planting remains limited, especially with the burgeoning need for residential and commercial infrastructure. Now, there are thousands of pocket gardens on rooftops and growing environments under the ground that are successful in growing plants which are then used for food.

"HYDROPONICS" is the growing of plants in a liquid nutrient solution with or without the use of artificial media. Commonly used mediums include expanded clay, coir, perlite, vermiculite, brick shards, polystyrene packing peanuts and wood fiber. Hydroponics has been recognized as a viable method of producing vegetables (tomatoes, lettuce, cucumbers and peppers) as well as ornamental crops such as herbs, roses, freesia and foliage plants. Due to the ban on methyl bromide in soil culture, the demand for hydroponically grown produce has rapidly increased in the last few years.

The roots may be flooded with the nutrient solution, or suspended in it. Others use systems wherein the roots are misted with the solution. Because of hydrophonics indoor gardens can now thrive in locations where the condition of the soil or the climate is inhospitable to growing plants. People and organizations that are intent on raising their own crops and living a more sustainable existence now have access to this kind of technology. Studies have shown that a general hydrophonics environment can produce even higher yields that traditional methods of growing crops.

AVAILABLE RESOURCES

In order to get started, it is necessary to have a hydrophonics kit from a dependable supplier. A regular multi-plant kit from a local source is compact and not that versatile, but it fulfills the basic requirements. There are better and more versatile hydro systems available from companies that are pioneers and specialists in the niche.

General hydro supplies usually include a growing tent, inline fans, filters, and lighting equipment. Online stores that offer a complete array of hydrophonic equipment make it easy for gardeners and farmers to make inquiries about hydro systems, purchase equipment, and ask for pertinent advice.

For millennia, traditional farming systems have proven to be reliable and dependable methods of producing food for the human race. However, now that agriculture faces significant challenges due to lack of space and climate change, hydrophonics can perhaps fill in the gaps in food production. After all, hydro systems allow people to grow various species of plants in locations that are not possible with traditional planting methods.

ADVANTAGES

Growing with hydroponics comes with many advantages, the biggest of which is a greatly increased rate of growth in your plants. With the proper setup, your plants will mature up to 25% faster and produce up to 30% more than the same plants grown in soil.

Your plants will grow bigger and faster because they will not have to work as hard to obtain nutrients. Even a small root system will provide the plant exactly what it needs, so the plant will focus more on growing upstairs instead of expanding the root system downstairs.

All of this is possible through careful control of your nutrient solution and pH levels. A hydroponic system will also use less water than soil based plants because the system is enclosed, which results in less evaporation. Believe it or not, hydroponics is better for the environment because it reduces waste and pollution from soil runoff.

- It can be used in places where in-ground agriculture or gardening is not possible (for example, dry desert areas or cold climate regions).

- More complete control of nutrient content, pH and growing environment.

- Lower water and nutrient costs associated with water and nutrient recycling.

- Faster growth due to more available oxygen in root area.

- Elimination or reduction of soil related insects, fungi and bacteria.

- Much higher crop yields.

- No weeding or cultivation required.

- Some crops, such as lettuce and strawberries, can be lifted from ground level to a much better height for planting, cultivation and harvesting. This gives much better working conditions and hence lowers labor costs.

- Crop rotation/fallowing is not necessary.

- Transplant shock is reduced.

DISADVANTAGES

Despite the fact that a hydroponics system has so many advantages, there are actually a few disadvantages as well. The biggest factor for most people is that a quality hydroponics system of any size will cost more than its soil counterpart. Then again, dirt isn't exactly expensive and you get what you pay for.

A large scale hydroponics system can take a lot of time to setup if you aren't the most experienced grower. Plus, managing your hydroponics system will take a lot of time as well. You will have to monitor and balance your pH and nutrient levels on a daily basis.

The greatest risk with a hydroponics system is that something like a pump failure can kill off your plants within hours depending on the size of your system. They can die quickly because the growing medium can't store water like soil can, so the plants are dependent on a fresh supply of water.

CHAPTER 2
CHOOSING HYDROPONICS MEDIUM

In hydroponics, the growing medium takes the place of the dirt/soil. Not to provide nutrients, but so the roots can support the plants weight and hold it upright. Just about any inert material can be used as a growing media. Inert meaning that it can't/won't decay or break down quickly, thus providing nutrients to the plants. Hydroponic growing media is simply a soil-less material that is generally porous so it can hold the moisture and oxygen that the root system requires to grow. Non porous materials can be used as well, but watering cycles would need to be more frequent so the roots don't dry out between waterings. The growing medium won't be able to grow anything on its own. If you placed plants in hydroponic growing media, and watered it with plain water, the plants would starve from nutrient deficiency. It's simply there to help support the plants weight as well as the moisture and oxygen the roots need. The nutrients the plants need, are provided by the nutrient solution, and is what the growing media is watered and moistened with. Some of the most widely used growing media's include Rockwool, Lightweight Expanded Clay Aggregate (called Hydroton), Coconut Fibre/Coconut chips, and Perlite or Vermiculite. While there are a lot of materials that can be used as growing media in hydroponics, they can all have very different properties than another type of media. We have even seen the use of hay bales as growing medium to grow tomatoes, using a drip lines on top to drip the nutrient solution onto the hay bales and tomato plant roots. There isn't one growing media that is better than the rest. Especially with so many different hydroponic system designs possible. However many growers eventually favour one type over others. There are a lot of things to consider when choosing what to use as a growing media. The type of system you're growing in and how you design and build that system is the biggest factor. While there is no one best growing media for all situations, some growing media's work better than others in different systems. With any hydroponic system, and/or any type of growing media, the goal is still the same. You just need the roots to be moist, not soggy and saturated. If the growing media is saturated and soggy, the roots will suffocate from lack of oxygen. That situation can easily lead to roots dying, and root rot. Although growing hydroponically is soil-free, this doesn't mean that there is nothing to support our plants. In most hydroponic systems, growers use different types of hydroponic media to help support their roots and maintain a good water/oxygen ratio.

In this guide, I'll give you a breakdown of the most popular types of hydroponic growing media. Every hydroponic gardener has their own preferences, so I'll give you the advantages and disadvantages of each medium so you can choose the one that works right for your situation.

COCO PEAT/COCO COIR

WHAT IS COCO COIR?

Coco coir is quickly becoming a favorite among hydroponic gardeners. It's made from ground up coconut husks and represents a giant leap in hydroponic growing media.

To understand why ground coconut husks are becoming so popular, let's take a look at what a coconut husk does for a coconut. Coconuts are grown in tropical regions, and often times they fall into the ocean when they are ripe. The husk protects the seed and flesh from sun and salt damage. Most importantly, the husk acts as a great growing medium for the coconut to germinate and create new trees.

Now apply these benefits to hydroponics. The ground up coco coir will act as a great hormone rich and fungus free medium for our plants. In the same way that it helps the coconut to germinate, it will help all of our seeds and seedlings to start strong. Coco coir has a great air to water ratio, so we don't have to worry about drowning our roots. Best of all, it's completely renewable. Coconut husks would generally go to waste or be composted if they weren't used in hydroponic applications. Here, we're taking what was once a waste product and re-purposing it to grow more plants!

HOW IS COCO COIR MADE?

To get coconut coir ready for hydroponic and gardening uses, it needs to go through extensive processing.

First, they need to remove the coir from the coconuts. This is done by soaking the husks in water to loosen and soften them. This is either done in tidal waters or freshwater. If done in tidal waters, the coconut coir will take up a large amount of salt, which will need to be flushed out by the manufacturer at a later stage.

Then, they're removed from the water bath and dried for over a year. After the drying process, which is quite extensive, the coir is organized into bales. These bales are then chopped and processed into various formats, from chips, to "croutons", to classic ground coconut coir.

There's a whole lot more that goes into the process of making coco coir safe and optimal for horticultural use.

PROS AND CONS TO COCONUT COIR

There are amazing benefits to using coconut coir in your garden. But just like any other kind of growing media, there are also some downsides to consider before you buy

BENEFITS OF COCO COIR

Good transition from soil gardening - growing in coco coir feels like growing in soil, because the two media look so similar. You can have a completely hydroponic garden that looks almost the same as a soil garden. The only difference is instead of watering with only water, you'd water your coconut coir garden with nutrient-enriched water.

Retains moisture and provides a good environment - coco coir is one of the most effective growing media for water retention out there. It can absorb up to 10x its weight in water, meaning the roots of your plants will never get dehydrated. There's also a lot of growing media for roots to work through, promoting healthy root development.

Environmentally safe - although I am a fan of using sphagnum peat moss in the garden, there's no denying the environmental concerns that peat moss poses. Coconut coir doesn't have the same problems. It can be used more than once unlike peat moss, which breaks down over time. It's also a repurposed waste product from a renewable resource, unlike the peat bogs where we get our peat moss.

Insect-neutral - most garden pests do not enjoy settling in coconut coir, making it yet another line of defense in your integrated pest management system for your garden.

Can be less complex than "traditional hydroponics" - if growing hydroponically is new to you, coconut coir is a good first step. You can practice the basics of hydroponic gardening without having to buy or build a hydroponic system and perform all of the maintenance that it requires.

DOWNSIDES TO COCO COIR

Inert - coconut coir is inert, meaning that it has no nutrients within it. It may look like soil, but it is not soil. This means you will need to add hydroponic nutrients and control the pH when using coco coir. Growing in soil isn't too different though, as many gardeners amend their soil constantly throughout the growing season anyways.

May need additional supplementation - you may find your plants short on calcium and magnesium when using coconut coir, so supplementing with "Cal-Mag" may be necessary.

Needs rehydration - most coco coir products are shipped in dry, compressed bricks. While this saves on shipping cost, it adds labor to your growing process as you'll need to rehydrate them before you can use them in the garden. This isn't too hard though!

Mixes can be expensive - garden suppliers know that coco coir can be annoying to work with sometimes, so they've started to offer coconut coir mixes. This saves a lot of time, but is pretty expensive — and making your own mix isn't too difficult.

TYPES OF COCO COIR

When you buy a coconut coir product, you're really buying three types of coconut coir: the fiber, the pith (or coconut peat), or the coco chips.

Together, they provide a powerful growing medium. Apart, they have very specific benefits. Here's a look at what each of them are.

COCO PITH OR COCO PEAT

The "peat" of coconut coir, this basically looks like finely ground coconut or peat moss. It's so small and absorbent that if you were to use coco peat as your only growing medium, you might drown out the roots of your plants. It must be aged properly to be used as a growing media, as it can let out salts that will kill your plant if you're not careful. Choosing a coconut coir manufacturer that ages properly is thus crucial for good growing.

COCO FIBER

Coconut fiber adds air pockets into your medium. It's not very absorbent, which is good because your growing media needs air pockets in order to provide oxygen to the root zone. Coconut fibers do break down rather quickly though, meaning the air pockets they create will also decrease over time.

COCO CHIPS

Coconut chips are basically an natural type of expanded clay pellet. They're just made from plant matter instead of clay! They are best thought of as a hybrid between coco peat and coco fiber. They're large enough to create air pockets, but also absorb water so your plants won't dehydrate completely.

When using coconut coir in the garden, it is vital that you use the right mixture of these three types for the best results.

HOW TO CHOOSE HIGH QUALITY COCO COIR

The most important factors in high quality coco coir is how it is harvested, prepared, and processed. Because none of these factors are directly in your control, you have to pick suppliers that follow all of the best practices for coco coir production.

After the coir is separated from the coconuts, it's stored in piles for a few years. This puts it at risk for pathogens due to the natural pH of coco coir. Most producers that experience this will chemically sterilize the coir so it's ready for use in your garden. This has its risks as well — it can prematurely break down the fibers and peat.

The absolute best manufacturers of coconut coir will have an iron-grip on their product from harvest to shipping.

THEY WILL:

Avoid situations that are conducive to pathogen growth

Have a dedicated system to control how the coconut coir ages

Rinse and wash the coir to flush out salts

Create the right blend of pith, fibers, and chips

Package and store their product correctly

If that sounds like a lot to look out for...IT IS! Fortunately, you don't have to do any of that. All you have to do is make sure that it was done, either by asking your local garden shop about the supplier's practices, or by reading on below where I've answered most of these questions for you for each type of coconut coir product I review.

THE BEST COCO COIR FOR YOUR GARDEN

Now that you have an understanding of what coco coir is, how it's processed and made, and what to look for when buying it, you're armed with the info you need to make a good buying decision.

We've tested a lot of different brands and learned a lot simply through trial and error. Here are our findings, which you can take with a grain of salt (pun intended).

WHAT NUTRIENTS DO YOU NEED FOR COCONUT COIR?

Because coconut coir is an inert growing media, you will need to supplement your plants with additional nutrition. Remember — this is still hydroponic growing if you are only using coconut coir.

While many people say you need coco coir-specific nutrients, this isn't absolutely necessary. You can get away with the standard General Hydroponics Flora series, a pH testing kit, and some Calimagic calcium + magnesium supplement.

If you want to mix it up and try something more coco coir specific, there are two options for you to try. These may be good options to pair with the matching coconut coir brand you've purchased:

CANNA Coco A + B + Calimagic

Fox Farms Nutrient Trio + Calimagic

GROWING TIPS

When coupled with fabric pots moisture problems can be avoided.

Built up salts can often be a problem, but there are many lines made particularly for coco that allow for easier flushing. Try using Canna Coco and Smart Pots.

BENEFITS OF COCONUT COIR

Usually organic

Sustainable

Compactable (buy compressed, expand at home...saves money on shipping)

DOWNSIDES OF COCONUT COIR

Holds a lot of water and may drown plants

EXPANDED CLAY PELLETS

WHAT ARE EXPANDED CLAY PELLETS?

Arguably one of the most popular media to use in days past has been hydroton expanded clay pellets. As their name suggests, these are made by expanding clay to form round balls of porous material. The best part about them is the fact that they release almost no nutrients into the water stream and are pH neutral. In addition, their spherical shape and porousness help to ensure a good oxygen/water balance so as not to overly dry or drown the roots.

In my experience, the only two downsides to using hydroton pellets has been their weight and their draining ability. In certain hydroponic systems, like ebb and flow, filling up an entire flood table full of hydroton is going to leave you with a very heavy system. They also drain and dry out very fast because there is much more space between each pellet than other hydroponic growing media. They can be used to great effect to line the bottom of an growing tray, when draining is an issue. Other than these two disadvantages, hydroton pellets are a great, re-usable media to use!

BENEFITS OF EXPANDED CLAY PELLETS

Reusable

pH Neutral

Do not compact

DOWNSIDE OF EXPANDED CLAY PELLETS

Heavy Drain and dry very fast, roots may dry out

Strip mined (environmental concerns)

OASIS CUBES

Oasis Cubes are similar to Rockwool cubes, and have similar property's. But oasis cubes are more like the rigid green or white floral foam used by forests to hold the stems in their flower displays. Oasis cubes are an open cell material which means that the cells can absorb water and air. The open cells wick moisture throughout the material, and the roots can easily grow and expand through the open cell structure. While oasis cubes are usually used as starter cubes for hydroponically grown plants, they also have bags you can fill your growing containers with. While oasis cubes are similar to rockwool, Oasis cubes don't become waterlogged as easily as rockwool cubes. Even so don't let it stay in constant contact with the water supply, or you'll still have water logging issues.

BENEFITS OF SURE TO GROW

Roots embed deeply into the medium and the plants and medium become one.

DOWNSIDES OF SURE TO GROW

Expensive, not re-usable

Need to have a top layer that stays 100% dry or it promotes algae growth.

PERLITE

Perlite is mainly composed of minerals that are subjected to very high heat, which then expand it like popcorn so it becomes very light weight, porous and absorbent. Perlite has a neutral pH, excellent wicking action, and is very porous. Perlite can by used by itself, or mixed with other types of growing media's. However because perlite is so light that it floats, depending on how you designed your hydroponic system, perlite by itself may not be the best choice of growing media for flood and drain systems.

Perlite is widely used in potting soils, and any nursery should carry bags of it. However perlite is sometimes also used as an additive added to cement. You may find it for a better price with the building supply's, and/or at places that sell concrete mixes and mixing supply's. When working with perlite be careful not to get any of the dust in your eyes. Rince it off to wash out the dust, and wet it down before working with it to keep the dust from going airborn.

Perlite is something that many traditional soil gardeners already recognize. It's a soil-free growing medium that has helped to add aeration to soil mixes for years. It's created by air-puffing volcanic glass to create an extremely light and porous material. It has one of the best oxygen retention levels of all growing media because of how porous it is.

Its weight can be a downside in certain hydroponic systems where water interacts directly with the growing media, causing it to shift around and wash away. Because of this, perlite is rarely ever used alone - typically it is mixed with coco coir, soil, or vermiculite.

BENEFITS OF PERLITE

Lightweight

High oxygen retention level

DOWNSIDES OF PERLITE

Too lightweight for certain hydroponic systems

Strip mined (environmental concerns)

Potential particle inhalation danger

GROWING TIPS

Straight perlite growing is one of the tried and true methods of hydroponic production. With virtually no cation exchange this media is a great option for longer term crops; especially in drain-to-waste scenarios. You have to watch out for moisture deficiencies as it holds absolutely no water!

STARTER PLUGS

WHAT ARE STARTER PLUGS?

A new and innovative entry into the hydroponic media space is what I will call a sponge start. It's made up of organic compost and doesn't break apart like soil due to a biodegradable binding material.

For those who are concerned about sustainability and organics, sponge starts are a great way to start seeds and incorporate them into your hydroponics system. I use these extensively for my seedlings and clones and I have to say that they are the most convenient and simple way to start out large quantities of new plants. You simply place them in trays and the roots grow straight downward towards the opening in the tray at the bottom. This is helpful when transplanting into any type of hydroponic system, where roots growing out to the sides aren't as beneficial.

BENEFITS OF STARTER PLUGS

Compact

Great for starting seeds

Relatively sustainable

DOWNSIDES OF STARTER PLUGS

Only suitable for starting seeds or cloning

Expensive

GROWING TIPS

If they remain wet and fungus gnats are a problem in your area, the gnats will infect the plugs.

ROCKWOOL

WHAT IS ROCKWOOL?

Rockwool is one of the most common growing media's used in hydroponics. Rockwool is a sterile, porous, non degradable medium that is composed primarily of granite and/or limestone which is super heated and melted, then spun into a small threads like cotton candy. The rockwool is then formed into blocks, sheets, cubes, slabs, or flocking. Rockwool sucks up water easily so you'll want to be careful not to let it become saturated, or it could suffocate your plants roots, as well as lead to stem rot and root rot. Rockwool should be pH balanced before use. That's done by soaking it in pH balanced water before use.

Rockwool has been around for decades and is well-known in the hydroponic growing community. It is made by melting rock and spinning it into extremely thin and long fibers, similar to fiberglass. They take these fibers and press them into cubes of varying sizes.

Rockwool has all of the benefits of most growing media, with some pretty serious downsides. It's not easy to dispose of - thin fibers of melted rock will last essentially forever when disposed of. Additionally, they usually come at a high pH and need soaking. The fibers and dust created in the spinning and compressing process can be harmful to eyes, nose and lungs. You can prevent the dust by immediately soaking rockwool in water once you take it out of the package. Because of these downsides, rockwool is rapidly being replaced by starter plugs as a reliable way to get seeds sprouting in your garden.

BENEFITS OF ROCKWOOL

Great water retention

Easy to dispose of

DOWNSIDES

The Danger of Rockwool

GROWSTONES

Growstones are made from recycled glass. They are similar to grow rocks (hydrocorn) but are made of clay and shaped marbles. Growstones are light weight, unevenly shaped, porous, and reusable, they provide good aeration and moisture to the root zone. They have good wicking ability and can wick water up to 4 inches above the water line. So you'll want to make sure it has good drainage or is deep enough so it doesn't wick water all the way to the top. Otherwise like with the growing media in any hydroponic system, if the top of the growing media is continually wet, you may have problems with stem rot. While they are made from recycled glass, their not sharp and you wont get cut from it, even if they break.

It bubbles and then they cool the mixture and break it up to form what looks like lava rocks. It's extremely lightweight, sustainable, and a great medium in almost any application. The one downside I"ve run into is that you typically can't reuse it because roots will stick to it after harvest and ruin sterility.

BENEFITS OF GROWSTONES

Lightweight

Great air to water ratio

Sustainable

DOWNSIDES OF GROWSTONES

Hard to clean

"One disadvantage is that due to their irregular sizes is that you have to mound more of them up to prevent light from entering your reservoir. Also if you tend to move plants from one medium or grow area to another as they get larger (like I do), Growstones tend to grip the plant roots too much and cause root damage. For this reason they are best used in a permanent grow bed."

RICE HULLS

WHAT ARE RICE HULLS?

Depending on your location, rice hulls may be readily available. It's a byproduct of the rice industry. Even though they are an organic plant material, they break down very slowly like coco coir, making them suitable as a growing media for hydroponics. Rice hulls are referred to as either fresh, aged, composted and parboiled, or carbonized. Fresh rice hulls are typically avoided as a hydroponic growing media because of the high probability of contaminants such as rice, fungal spores, bacteria, decaying bugs, and weed seeds. Parboiled rice hulls (PRH) is done by stemming and drying the rice hulls after the rice has been milled from them. This kills any spores, bacteria, and microorganisms, leaving a sterile and clean product.

Rice hulls are also often used as part of a mix of growing media such as 30%-40% rice hulls and pine bark mix. The overall pH of parboiled and composted rice hulls range from 5.7 to 6.5, which is right in the pH range for most hydroponically grown plants. Fresh and/or composted rice hulls tend to have a high Manganese (Mn) content. But problems with Manganese toxicity can be avoided as long as the pH is above 5. Which is below normal range for hydroponics anyway.

These are the shells that surround rice. They allow for good drainage and retain little water in general. Rice hulls are a product that would normally be thrown away, so putting them to extra use in hydroponics re-purposes something that would otherwise be thrown away.

BENEFITS OF RICE HULLS

Makes use of a byproduct that would otherwise be wasted

Retains little water

DOWNSIDES OF RICE HULLS

Decays over time

PUMICE

What is Pumice?

Very similar to perlite. Lightweight mineral that is crushed and used in some hydroponics systems.

BENEFITS OF PUMICE

Lightweight

High oxygen retention level

DOWNSIDES OF PUMICE

Too lightweight for some hydroponic systems if bought as small pieces

SAND

WHAT IS SAND?

Sand Is actually a very common growing media used in hydroponics. It's the main growing media used at the Epcot Center Hydroponic Greenhouse in Florida. Mainly for their large hydroponically grown plants and trees. Sand is like rock, just smaller in size. Because the particle size is smaller than regular rock, moisture doesn't drain out as fast. Sand is also commonly mixed with Vermiculite, Perlite, and or coco coir. All help retain moisture as well as help aerate the mix for the roots.

When using sand as a growing media you will want to use the largest grain size you can get. That will help increase aeration to the roots by increasing the size of the air pockets between the grains of sand. Mixing Vermiculite, Perlite, and or coco coir with the sand will also help aerate. You will also want to rinse the sand well before use to get as much of the dust particles out of it as you can. One big downside to using sand as a growing media for hydroponics is that it is very heavy. 3-4 gallons of wet sand can weigh up to 50lbs. So you won't want to be moving it once you get it set up. Or use it in a ratio of something like 20%-30% sand and the rest Vermiculite, Perlite, or another type of growing media to reduce weight. One of the most plentiful types of media on the planet! Sand is extremely cheap (or free!) Sand is cheap and easily available. It's a great way to get started, but it is fairly heavy, must be sterilized often, and has low water retention. Arguably the oldest hydroponic media, holds no water or nutrient load and can exacerbate deficiencies quickly.

BENEFITS OF SAND

Cheap

Easy to find

DOWNSIDES OF SAND

Heavy

Low water retention

Small size may affect certain hydroponic systems

GRAVEL

WHAT IS GRAVEL?

This is the same material that is used in aquariums. As long as it is washed, you can use any type of gravel. Relatively cheap and easy to clean. A great DIY starter media if you're short on cash!

BENEFITS OF GRAVEL

Very inexpensive Easy to clean Drains well

DOWNSIDES OF GRAVEL

Heavy Plant roots may dry out Not suitable for certain hydroponic systems

GRAVEL GROWING TIPS

Works very well as long as it is not in contact with the water or it can cause PH swings. Great medium because it is cheap and readily available. It can be reused but due to their small size, it is common that they get very tangled in the plant roots which makes it not worth removing and cleaning since it is already so cheap.

WOOD FIBER

WHAT IS WOOD FIBER?

Simply wood. Great and efficient media for hydroponics. If you want to go truly organic with your growing media...you can't get any better than wood chips! Additionally, some studies have indicated that wood chips reduce the effect of plant growth regulators, meaning your plants may grow slightly larger.

BENEFITS OF WOOD FIBER

Organic

Holds structure for a long time

DOWNSIDES OF WOOD FIBER

Biodegradable

May not be sterile

May attract pests

BRICK SHARDS

WHAT ARE BRICK SHARDS?

Name says it all: crushed up bricks. Very similar in effect to gravel. However, they may affect the pH as they are not pH neutral, and also require extra cleaning to get rid of brick dust.

BENEFITS OF BRICK SHARDS

Inexpensive

Easy to clean

Drains well

DOWNSIDES

May affect pH

Requires more thorough cleaning

Heavy

Plant roots may dry out

POLYSTYRENE PACKING PEANUTS

WHAT ARE POLYSTYRENE PACKING PEANUTS?

These are the standard packing peanuts used in the shipping industry. They're cheap, available everywhere, and drain fairly well. Tough to use uncovered outdoor due to their light weight...the typical use is in Nutrient Film Technique systems. There is the possibility that plants will absorb styrene, so these may pose a contamination risk.

BENEFITS OF PACKING PEANUTS

Cheap (often free)

Very lightweight

Drain well

DOWNSIDES OF PACKING PEANUTS

Only polystyrene will work - biodegradable packing peanuts will turn to slush

Potential for plants to absorb styrene

VERMICULITE

WHAT IS VERMICULITE?

Vermiculite is a silicate mineral that like perlite, expands when exposed to very high heat. As a growing media, vermiculite is quite similar to perlite except that it has a relatively high cation-exchange capacity, meaning it can hold nutrients for later use. Also like the perlite, vermiculite is very light and tends to float. There are different uses and types of vermiculite, so you'll want to be sure what you get is intended for horticulture use. The easiest way to be sure is to get it from a nursery.

Vermiculite very similar to Perlite. It's a mineral that is heated until it expands into pebbles. It retains more water than perlite and can wick (draw) water and nutrients upwards. Often used in combination with other types of media to create a highly customized media for specific hydroponic applications.

BENEFITS OF VERMICULITE

Water retention

DOWNSIDES

Hard to find

Expensive

Can hold too much water

CHAPTER 3
TYPES OF HYDROPONIC SYSTEM

The cool thing about hydroponics is that there are many different types of hydroponics systems available. Some of the best hydroponic systems on the market combine different types of hydroponics into one hybrid hydroponic system. Hydroponics is unique in that there are multiple techniques you can use to get the nutrient solution to your plants.

DEEPWATER CULTURE

Deepwater CultureDeepwater Culture (DWC), also known as the reservoir method, is by far the easiest method for growing plants with hydroponics. In a Deepwater Culture hydroponic system, the roots are suspended in a nutrient solution. An aquarium air pump oxygenates the nutrient solution, this keeps the roots of the plants from drowning. Remember to prevent light from penetrating your system, as this can cause algae to grow. This will wreak havoc on your system.

The primary benefit to using a Deepwater Culture system is that there are no drip or spray emitters to clog. This makes DWC an excellent choice for organic hydroponics, as hydroponics systems that use organic nutrients are more prone to clogs.

NUTRIENT FILM TECHNIQUE

Nutrient Film TechniqueNutrient Film Techinque, or NFT, is a type of hydroponic system where a continous flow of nutrient solution runs over the plants roots. This type of solution is on a slight tilt so that the nutrient solution will flow with the force of gravity.

This type of system works very well because the roots of a plant absorb more oxygen from the air than from the nutrient solution itself. Since only the tips of the roots come in contact with the nutrient solution, the plant is able to get more oxygen which fascilitates a faster rate of growth.

AEROPONICS

Aerogarden Aeroponics SystemAeroponics is a hydroponics method by which the roots are misted with a nutrient solution while suspended in the air. There are two primary methods to get the solution to the exposed roots. The first method involves a fine spray nozzle to mist the roots. The second method uses what's called a pond fogger. If you decide to use a pond fogger then make sure you use a Teflon coated disc, as this will reduce the amount of maintenance required.

You may have heard of the AeroGarden, which is a commercialized aeroponics system. The AeroGarden is an excellent entry point to aeroponics. It's a turn-key system that requires little setup. It also comes with great support and supplies to get you started.

WICKING

Hydroponic Wick SystemWicking is one of the easiest and lowest costing methods of hydroponics. The concept behind wicking is that you have a material, such as cotton, that is surrounded by a growing medium with one end of the wick material placed in the nutrient solution. The solution is then wicked to the roots of the plant.

This system can be simplified by removing the wick material all together and just using a medium that has the ability to wick nutrients to the roots. This works by suspending the bottom of your medium directly in the solution. We recommend using a medium such as perlite or vermiculite. Avoid using mediums such as Rockwool, coconut coir, or peat moss because they may absorb too much of your nutrient solution which can suffocate the plant.

EBB & FLOW

Ebb and Flow SystemAn ebb & flow hydroponics system, also known as a flood and drain system, is a great system for growing plants with hydroponics. This type of system functions by flooding the growing area with the nutrient solution at specific intervals. The nutrient solution then slowly drains back into the reservoir. The pump is hooked to a timer, so the process repeats itself at specific intervals so that your plants get the desired amount of nutrients.

An ebb & flow hydroponics system is ideal for plants that are accustomed to periods of dryness. Certain plants flourish when they go through a slight dry period because it causes the root system to grow larger in search of moisture. As the root system grows larger the plant grows faster because it can absorb more nutrients.

DRIP SYSTEM

Drip SystemA hydroponic drip system is rather simple. A drip system works by providing a slow feed of nutrient solution to the hydroponics medium. We recommend using a slow draining medium, such as Rockwool, coconut coir, or peat moss. You can also use a faster draining medium, although you will have to use a faster dripping emitter.

The downside to a system like this is that the drippers / emitter are famous for clogging. We prefer not to use drip systems, but it can be an effective method for growing if you can avoid the clogs that plague this type of system. The reason the system gets clogged is because particles from nutrients that build up in the emitter. Systems that use organic nutrients are more likely to have this kind of issue.

CHAPTER 4
PLANT NUTRITION

Hydroponics cultivation is considered to be superior to conventional cultivation because of the many advantages it offers. For both commercial and small scale crop cultivation, hydroponics techniques have proved to have advantages in many areas. One of the advantages hydroponics offers is its simplicity. However, what is a fairly simple and straight forward technique can seem complicated at times, especially to beginners. This is especially true when it comes to the issue of plant nutrition. Given the countless number of tonics, additives, growth enhancers, accelerators, and other concoctions that promise accelerated growth, bigger yields and so on, this basic aspect of hydroponics can seem frustratingly complicated. The good news is that with a little reading and hands-on experience, it isn't. Following a good nutrient schedule and keeping it simple will go a long way, ensuring proper uptake of all essential nutrients. It is best not to use too many products as it may be very difficult to trace the exact cause of the problem if there are many additives and supplements in the nutrient mix.

NUTRIENT FORMULATIONS

All plants, whether they are grown in soil or with hydroponics require a balance of nitrogen, phosphorous, potassium (N-P-K), and other macro and/or micro (trace) elements to grow properly. These nutrients are available to plants in soil in small unknown amounts, but over time they get depleted and need to be supplied separately to make up for the deficiency. In hydroponics, it is all the more important to be sure that plants are getting the right nutrients in the right amounts at the right times. Hydroponic nutrient formulas are structured for specific stages of a plants life cycle. A plant's nutritional requirements change according to the stages of its life cycle. When plants are in the vegetative stage, they require greater amounts of nitrogen, which is the key element for the development of leaves and stems. A deficiency in nitrogen during the growth period leads to stunted growth with yellowing of leaves. This is the most commonly seen deficiency in plants. During the flowering cycle the plant requires less nitrogen, but more phosphorus and potassium. Using good quality nutrients that contain the vital elements for plant growth should be the first consideration in providing plant nutrition in hydroponics.

GROWTH ENHANCERS, BOOSTERS AND FORTIFIERS

Many products have been developed that can stimulate faster nutrient uptake and speed up stem, leaf, and flower/fruit growth. Many of these products are best left to the advanced and experienced growers. Novice growers should approach such products with caution. Several products available on the market work specifically as bloom fortifiers or enhancers. These formulations act to stimulate flowering and increase essential oils in plants. While selecting a bloom fortifier, the best thing to remember is to select one with a proper NPK ratio. Such fortifiers will generally have no nitrogen and are rich in phosphorus and potassium. These essential minerals stimulate the formation of super blooms.

ORGANIC FORMULATIONS

Organic gardening has become popular in recent years and the hydroponics industry has sought to integrate organic growing practices into hydroponic cultivation. Several organic products have been successfully developed, tested and marketed. Organic formulas for use in hydroponics should be soluble, stand-alone products that leave no sediment in the container. Make sure the organic formula can be used in hydroponics and does not require shaking prior to use. Any sediment in the formula will likely clog your tubing and water pumps. Organic formulas meant for soil cultivated plants are not suitable for use in hydroponics due to issues with clogged equipment, which will result in damage to your plants.

OTHER CONSIDERATIONS

Plants need to have fresh nutrients available for healthy growth. It is important to do regular reservoir changes every week. pH and electro conductivity (ppm) should be checked while mixing your nutrient solution. While the ppm reading will help determine the amount of dissolved nutrients, the pH reading will help in maintaining acid and alkalinity levels that will enable plants to absorb the nutrients. Flushing or rinsing should be carried out at least one to two weeks prior to harvest. This can be done using regular water or a flushing solution in your system to wash out excess salts that remain in the growing medium. Many people like to keep a gardening journal which will help in avoiding repeat mistakes and establish pointers to the right course of action. Overtime, making journal entries regularly will help build up a wealth of valuable information on various aspects of nutrition, pH, EC, etc., that are specific to you and your garden.

MACRO AND MICRO NUTRIENTS

MACRO-NUTRIENTS AND THEIR ROLE IN PLANT GROWTH

- Carbon- Formation of organic compounds

- Oxygen- Release of energy from sugar

- Hydrogen- Water formation

- Nitrogen- Chlorophyll, amino acids, proteins synthesis

- Phosphorus- Vital for photosynthesis and growth

- Potassium- Enzyme activity, Sugar and starch formation

- Calcium- Cell growth and division, component of cell wall

- Magnesium-Component of chlorophyll, enzyme activation

- Sulfur- Formation of amino acids and proteins

MICRO- NUTRIENTS AND THEIR ROLE IN PLANT GROWTH

- Boron – Vital for reproduction

- Chlorine – Helps root growth

- Copper- Enzyme activation

- Iron- Used in Photosynthesis

- Manganese- Component of chlorophyll, Enzyme activation

- Sodium- Vital for water movement

- Zinc- Component of enzymes and auxins

- Molybdenum- Nitrogen Fixation

- Nickel- Nitrogen Liberation

- Cobalt- Nitrogen Fixation

- Silicon- Cell wall toughness

CHAPTER 5
LIGHTING SOLUTION

Hydroponic gardening can take place indoors or outdoors. When growing plants indoors, prime growing conditions will require grow lights or artificial lighting to replace the absent sunlight.

ARTIFICIAL LIGHTING

Photosynthesis is the fundamental food making process in all green plants with light being the major component in the process. Photosynthesis is a process used by plants and other organisms to convert light energy, normally from the Sun, into chemical energy that can be later released to fuel the organisms' activities.

During daylight hours or lamp hours, the plant traps and stores light energy and then converts it into chemical energy. The light energy produced is determined by the color and the intensity of the light. Once the plant has stored its limit of light energy, it can no longer capture anymore and the accessed light goes to waste.

Too many grow lights can be harmful to the growth of your plants. The same applies if the plant doesn't receive the necessary amount of light. Not enough light results in the plant not having enough stored light energy or stored chemical energy to carry out its natural growth cycle.

This energy is stored in the leaf tissue. Therefore, the more area of the leaf that is exposed to the light the better. Plants experience their optimal growth using high intensity lighting and is optimized when the entire light spectrum is provided.

HYDROPONIC GROW LIGHTS

There are several different lighting options and configurations to choose from. At different stages of growth, your hydroponic vegetables' development can benefit from using different types of lighting. For example, while veggies are maturing and developing stems and leaves, a blue light spectrum lamp such as a Metal Halide (MH), is most beneficial. Then when the vegetables begin to form, a red light spectrum such as High Pressure Sodium Lamps (HPS) lamps, are the most effective. Changing the spectrum and lighting through different stages of growth works best and at times a blend of lighting will be ideal.

If you choose to use standard incandescent bulbs as your grow lights, your lighting set-up will also require cooling fans to keep the air around the plants moving and to prevent overheating. High Intensity Discharge (HID) lights create a lot of light without generating heat. Too much heat will prevent growth and healthy development of your plants so be sure to know what is required for your yield. Reflectors and ballasts will be needed to get the most energy out of your lamps.

LIGHT PLACEMENT

Indoor grow lighting. Image via Homemade Hydroponic Vegetables.

Indoor grow lighting. Image via Homemade Hydroponic Vegetables.

Placing your lighting correctly is essential to support your hydroponics vegetable growth. Plants don't benefit from lighting that is not directly on them. Seedlings like having lights hung directly over them, approximately 2-4 inches above the top of the plants. As the plants grow the lights can be adjusted and moved up to maintain their distance of 2-4 inches.

It may be surprising to believe, but fewer plants result in a larger yield. When there are too many plants they become crowded and compete for the available light.

The plant receiving the light will shade the other plant out which will result in every plant performing far below potential levels. Balance the numbers of plants with light availability for best results.

Start with fewer plants and then remove leaves that you see aren't getting the desired amount of light. When you remove the leaves it reduces the photosynthetic potential. All the leaves are used to store the light energy. When it's time to draw on that stored chemical energy, the energy needs to come from the full plant cycle.

If you start with proper lighting, your crops will end in producing maximum yields and will result in a highly successful harvest. The light cycle and light time plays a factor in the health of your plants.

CHAPTER 6
CONCLUSION

Hydroponic vegetable gardening is becoming not just the obvious choice for growers but also working out as a hobby for people who have interest in gardening. Hydroponic vegetable garden helps you grow your choice of fruit, flowers and vegetables. Hydroponics simply means growing plants with the aid of mineral nutrients solutions and not the soil. In Hydroponic vegetable gardening the plants roots are grown in inert growing medium like gravel, water, sand or even air etc. Let's learn some of the most hydroponic gardening secrets to make your own garden with quality and healthy crops and plants without any much effort. The roots of the vegetables grow largely to search for food and water. All the hydroponically grown plants can grow up taller and don't involve an extensive root system because their nutrients are readily available to the root system wherein it's not the case in soil medium in which the root extend itself much to get its basic nutrients requirements from the soil.

Hydroponic gardening is a more proficient way of growing vegetables than soil-based plants. Plants can grow drastically and effectively together even if they are grown close to each other in hydroponic vegetable gardens. Unlike in traditional agriculture system, where the plants need more gap because the soil create bigger roots for the plants.

In hydroponic vegetable gardening water acts as the reservoir or medium for the organic nutrients for the plants to absorb it. But researches state that only soil is not vital for the plant growth. The organic nutrients need to dissolve in water, so that the plants can absorb it. If the fundamental organic nutrients are provided to the vegetables through water in an artificial form, the plant then doesn't require soil for its growth. Therefore, hydroponic gardening are coming into picture for its very effective and useful cultivation technique that has brought about a great revolution in agricultural sector.

When you are planning to make hydroponic vegetable gardens, pick from a variety of types of containers available in the market, the type of hydroponic gardening supplies you will be using for your hydroponic garden. When gardening hydroponics there is no specific nutrient solutions are taken into account for the growth of the plants. Once the plant starts growing and start using the nutrients, composition may happen to change. Rockwool is known to be one of the most commonly used mediums for hydroponics gardening.

Hydroponics vegetable gardening helps the plant growth in every stage. You can grow crops to the advanced level in a very small area, allowing the crop turnaround time. Hydroponic gardening facilitates you with a whole new method of growing crops with a healthy and rich way. There will be larger no of plants and crops grown by the help of hydroponics vegetable gardens than with traditional way of growing crops. Also, the quality that you will get with the output grown by the help of hydroponics you won't get with old agricultural techniques.

In Hydroponics, the plants root are inundated in the water solution which is again a mixture or organic nutrients in a proper container or tray which have holes in it to put the plants in it. The roots are open and submerged in the water to get its required nutrients from it. Hence, Hydroponic vegetable gardening is making a very fast market than the traditional way of agricultural methods.

88969561R00026

Made in the USA
Lexington, KY
20 May 2018